The Rainy Day

Edited by Gillian Doherty
With thanks to Dr. Roger Brugge, from the Department of Meteorology,
Reading University, for information about clouds and rainy days

First published in 2005 by Usborne Publishing Ltd, 83-85 Saffron Hill, London EC1N 8RT, England.
www.usborne.com Copyright © 2005 Usborne Publishing Ltd. The name Usborne and the devices ♀ ⊕ are Trade Marks
 First published in America in 2005. UE. Printed in Dubai.

The Rainy Day

Anna Milbourne

Illustrated by Sarah Gill

Designed by Laura Fearn and Laura Parker

Big, dark clouds
are hiding the sun.

It looks like it's going
to be a rainy day.

Have you ever wondered
what clouds are made of?

Sometimes, they look as if
you could cuddle them.

But really, they're nothing but wispy mist.

Clouds are made of lots and lots of teeny-tiny water drops.

Inside the clouds, the water drops
grow bigger and **bigger**.

After a while, they grow so big and so heavy,

they fall

right out

of the sky...

and it starts to rain.

The rain falls softly at first.

Birds huddle in the trees
to keep their feathers dry.

Other animals hop and creep and crawl away to hide.

Then all at once...

it pours and pours.

The rain makes puddles
on the ground.

Splish

Splash

Splosh

Snails like being out in the rain.

Wriggly worms
love getting wet.

Frogs come out
to hop about...

and splash in
the puddles.

Plants like the rain too.

Rain trickles into the soil.

Thirsty plants suck it up
through their roots.

The sun peeps out
from behind the clouds...

and shines through the falling rain.

A beautiful rainbow appears in the sky.

red
orange
yellow
green
blue
indigo
violet

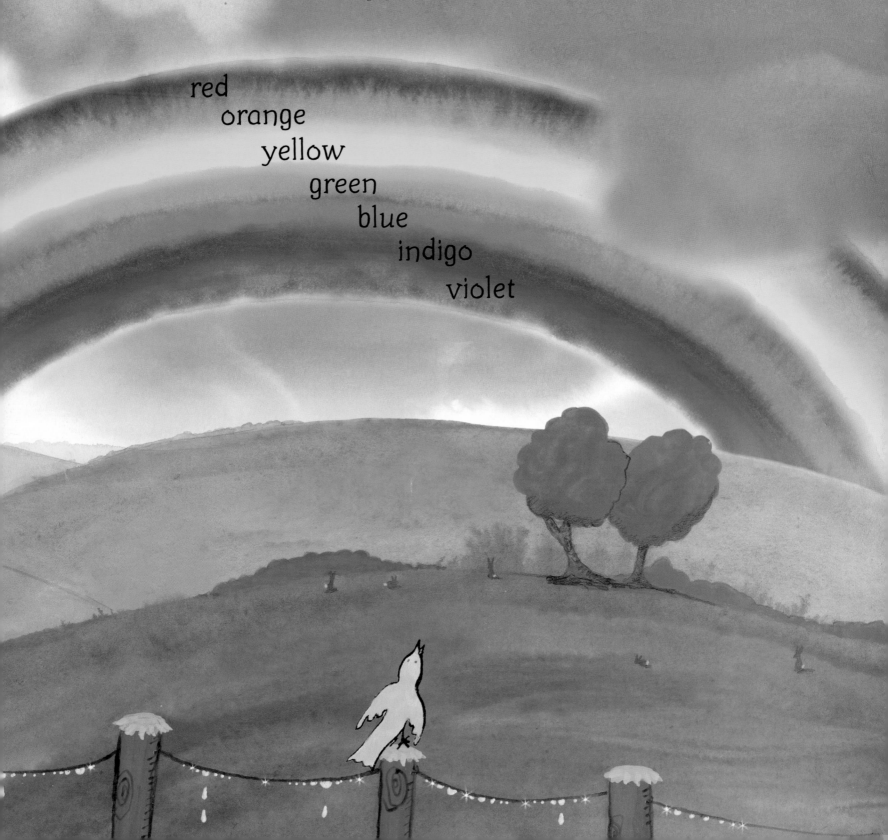

As the rain stops, the rainbow
gently fades away.

The clouds float away across the sky.

Squelch

Squelch

The ground has turned to squishy mud.

A thousand tiny raindrops
sparkle in the grass...

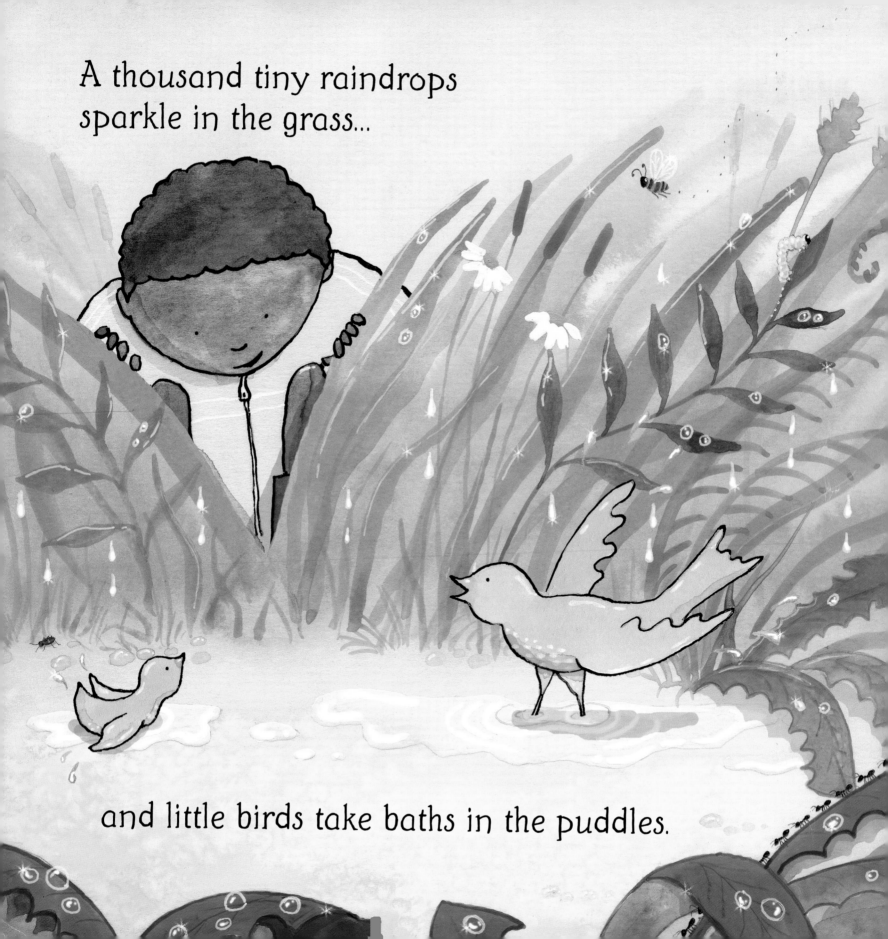

and little birds take baths in the puddles.

The warm sunshine
dries up all the rain.

Slowly, the puddles get smaller

and smaller

until they are all gone.

It looks like it's going
to be a sunny afternoon.